THE CHRISTMAS PRINCESS

A full-length fairy tale by
Arthur M. Jolly

www.youthplays.com
info@youthplays.com
424-703-5315

The Christmas Princess © 2005 Arthur M. Jolly
All rights reserved. ISBN 978-1-62088-008-1.

Caution: This play is fully protected under the copyright laws of the United States of America, Canada, the British Commonwealth and all other countries of the copyright union and is subject to royalty for all performances including but not limited to professional, amateur, charity and classroom whether admission is charged or presented free of charge.

Reservation of Rights: This play is the property of the author and all rights for its use are strictly reserved and must be licensed by his representative, YouthPLAYS. This prohibition of unauthorized professional and amateur stage presentations extends also to motion pictures, recitation, lecturing, public reading, radio broadcasting, television, video and the rights of adaptation or translation into non-English languages.

Performance Licensing and Royalty Payments: Amateur and stock performance rights are administered exclusively by YouthPLAYS. No amateur, stock or educational theatre groups or individuals may perform this play without securing authorization and royalty arrangements in advance from YouthPLAYS. Required royalty fees for performing this play are available online at www.YouthPLAYS.com. Royalty fees are subject to change without notice. Required royalties must be paid each time this play is performed and may not be transferred to any other performance entity. All licensing requests and inquiries should be addressed to YouthPLAYS.

Author Credit: All groups or individuals receiving permission to produce this play must give the author(s) credit in any and all advertisement and publicity relating to the production of this play. The author's billing must appear directly below the title on a separate line with no other accompanying written matter. The name of the author(s) must be at least 50% as large as the title of the play. No person or entity may receive larger or more prominent credit than that which is given to the author(s) and the name of the author(s) may not be abbreviated or otherwise altered from the form in which it appears in this Play.

Publisher Attribution: All programs, advertisements, flyers or other printed material must include the following notice:
Produced by special arrangement with YouthPLAYS (www.youthplays.com).

Prohibition of Unauthorized Copying: Any unauthorized copying of this book or excerpts from this book, whether by photocopying, scanning, video recording or any other means, is strictly prohibited by law. This book may only be copied by licensed productions with the purchase of a photocopy license, or with explicit permission from YouthPLAYS.

Trade Marks, Public Figures & Musical Works: This play may contain references to brand names or public figures. All references are intended only as parody or other legal means of expression. This play may also contain suggestions for the performance of a musical work (either in part or in whole). YouthPLAYS has not obtained performing rights of these works unless explicitly noted. The direction of such works is only a playwright's suggestion, and the play producer should obtain such permissions on their own. The website for the U.S. copyright office is *http://www.copyright.gov*.

COPYRIGHT RULES TO REMEMBER

1. To produce this play, you must receive prior written permission from YouthPLAYS and pay the required royalty.

2. You must pay a royalty each time the play is performed in the presence of audience members outside of the cast and crew. Royalties are due whether or not admission is charged, whether or not the play is presented for profit, for charity or for educational purposes, or whether or not anyone associated with the production is being paid.

3. No changes, including cuts or additions, are permitted to the script without written prior permission from YouthPLAYS.

4. Do not copy this book or any part of it without written permission from YouthPLAYS.

5. Credit to the author and YouthPLAYS are required on all programs and other promotional items associated with this play's performance.

When you pay royalties, you are recognizing the hard work that went into creating the play and making a statement that a play is something of value. We think this is important, and we hope that everyone will do the right thing, thus allowing playwrights to generate income and continue to create wonderful new works for the stage.

Plays are owned by the playwrights who wrote them. Violating a playwright's copyright is a very serious matter and violates both United States and international copyright law. Infringement is punishable by actual damages and attorneys' fees, statutory damages of up to $150,000 per incident, and even possible criminal sanctions. **Infringement is theft. Don't do it.**

Have a question about copyright? Please contact us by email at info@youthplays.com or by phone at 424-703-5315. When in doubt, please ask.

CAST OF CHARACTERS

THE FOOL, a clown, desperately bad at being a jester, her jokes fall flat, but physically comic. This role can be played M or F, with appropriate dialogue changes (he for she, etc.).

THE QUEEN, imperious.

THE KING, well meaning, but gruff.

THE PRINCESS, beautiful but spoiled rotten.

LUCY THE MAID, sensible, until she falls in love.

PRINCE VALIANT, handsome but dumb.

ALLAN, a rugged woodsman.

WAKENDA THE WITCH, a true witch, one that understands people.

THE CRESCENT MOON BEAR, big and scary. (Doubled by the King, though it is also possible for a different actor to play this role to create an additional casting opportunity.)

THE DRAGON, amplified voice for an outsize puppet. (Voiced by the Queen.) The puppet itself could be moved/danced by anywhere from a pair of dancers who also play the Woodland Sprites (in a small cast production) to a whole company of dancers (for instance, if it were a Chinese Dragon).

WOODLAND SPRITES, a dance ensemble of any size, dependent on the needs of the production.

SETTINGS

A Castle with two entrances, upstage left and upstage right.
A gloomy forest, with a witch's hovel and a bear's cave.

PROPS

Dragon, as big as possible (two-person costume or Chinese parade-dragon style).

A crystal vial on a necklace.

A cauldron, preferably over a fire.

A miniature cauldron.

An immense ball of string.

A crimson rose.

A portable Christmas tree covered in whipped cream.

PLAYWRIGHT'S NOTES

In previous productions, additional commedia dell'arte style lazzis have been added—a chase sequence with the Jester and the Prince on their way to the Princess' chambers, etc.

* The punchline on page 43, the third "sad thing" the Princess mentions, has been updated for every show, sometimes each performance, depending on the news of the day. "Not getting Hannah Montana tickets" was big one year, "Your wife bashing your Escalade with your own golf clubs" was another. Have fun with it.

ACKNOWLEDGMENTS

The Christmas Princess was first performed by the Coop Theatre Company at The Black Box Theatre in Santa Monica, California. December 17th, 2005.

Cast was as follows:

The JESTER	John Frank
The QUEEN	Janet Chamberlain
The KING	Robert Miano
The PRINCESS	Christy Buchholz

LUCY the MAID	Maura Kay
PRINCE VALIANT	Jason D. Avalos
Dancer/Puppeteer	Ericka Sance
Dancer/Puppeteer	Enissa Ann Harris
ALLAN	Scott Gerard
WAKENDA the WITCH	Dalia Vosylius
CRESCENT MOON BEAR	Luke Michael
The DRAGON	Janet Chamberlain

Directed by Jeni Bartiromo
Produced by Corey Shane Love
Costumes by Rachael Graeff
Set Design & Props by Sandy Von Guttenstein
Choreography by Monica Juodvalkis

PRE-SHOW

(THE FOOL, wearing a tricorn hat with bells on, helps audience members to their seats — with much humorous byplay — throwing of popcorn, etc.)

(As the houselights fade, she sits down in the aisle.)

(Lights up.)

SCENE 1—THE PALACE

(A long pause.)

FOOL: We want the show! We want the show! They're never going to start.

(She wanders on stage.)

Where are they all?   Why aren't they starting?   *(To AUDIENCE:)* Are you lot ready? ...Well, I'm ready. Which is good, because I start the show. I have the very first line, so I'm very important. *(She looks around:)* Come on! We're waiting! I'm brilliant, you know. I come on and I tell you all about the beautiful Princess, and how she's going to get married to a handsome prince tomorrow! On Christmas! He's as dumb as a bucket of rocks, but you can't have everything. When you're a Princess, you have to marry a prince. Or a frog. I read that in a book somewhere, you can marry a frog too. Not much of a choice, if you ask me. I mean, if someone asked you, would you rather marry a handsome prince who has quite a lot of money and lives in a huge castle with satellite TV and Nintendo RockBand Troubadour Edition, or marry a smelly, slimy frog that lives in a muddy pond and eats flies...it wouldn't be a hard decision, would it. Unless, you really, really like slime.   But the Princess doesn't want to marry someone she's never met. She says she doesn't love him. I told her, he may have all the personality of a cardboard box in the rain, but at least he doesn't eat flies. She doesn't listen to me. No one listens to me, and I'm the most important person here. I have the very first line in the show. When are they going to start? COME ON ALREADY! I'm going to go see what's going on.

(She exits at the Upstage Left Door. A CLANGING GONG sound.)

(From Offstage:) Oooh!

> *(She staggers back on stage through the Upstage Right Door, clasping her head.)*

They just explained it to me. I'm late! I should've started already. I better go see why I haven't started yet.

> *(She exits Upstage Left as the KING and QUEEN enter Upstage Right.)*

QUEEN: Where is she? Oh, that silly woman.

KING: Everyone's waiting.

QUEEN: I don't know why you hired her.

KING: She's a fool.

QUEEN: She's an idiot.

> *(The Fool runs on.)*

Where have you been? You should've started already.

FOOL: You started without me?

QUEEN: You weren't here.

FOOL: Where was I?

QUEEN: In the back.

FOOL: Oh my goodness! I'll run and get me.

> *(She runs on Up Left.)*

KING: The sad thing is, she thinks she's funny.

> *(The Fool runs on Up Right.)*

FOOL: I'm not back there! Go on without me.

QUEEN: Really, she's the worst jester anywhere. You must get rid of her.

FOOL: No!

KING: You're a terrible fool.   You haven't made me laugh once since I hired you.

FOOL: *(Desperately:)* I can make you laugh!   ...Uh...what's brown and sticky?

(The King and Queen look at each other.)

A stick!

QUEEN: You're an irritating little person. Harry, throw her in the dungeon.

FOOL: No, no! I can be funny. I can! What did—uh—what did the blind horse say to the parrot with one leg a little shorter than the other leg?

QUEEN: Hmmm...What <u>did</u> the blind horse say to the parrot with one leg a little shorter than the other leg?

KING: Yes, what did the blind horse say to the parrot with one leg a little shorter than the other leg?

(Beat.)

FOOL: I have no idea. I was just desperately hoping I'd think of something.

KING: Tomorrow is Christmas day—and our beautiful daughter will be marrying Prince Valiant. It will be the finest wedding ever—a Christmas wedding. It will be a perfect day. And as Court Jester, your job is to be funny. If you have not made me laugh by the time the wedding is over, I will drop you in the deepest, darkest, nastiest, moldiest dungeon in the castle!

FOOL: Why sirrah, I will make you laugh...I will...uh...*(To the youngest, littlest girl in the front row:)* Do you know any jokes?

(Reaction. Improvisation.)

(Joke or not, eventually the Fool turns to the King.)

She's not making you laugh either. Throw her in the dungeon!

KING: OUT! AWAY WITH YOU!

(Quaking, the Fool runs off.)

QUEEN: Come, we have so much to prepare for the wedding tomorrow.

(They exit. Blackout.)

SCENE 2 — ANOTHER PART OF THE PALACE
(PRINCESS' CHAMBERS)

(The PRINCESS sits at a mirror. LUCY, her maid, combs the Princess' hair.)

LUCY: Ninety-six,   ninety-seven,   ninety-eight,   ninety-nine...one hundred. There.

PRINCESS: Am I not the most beautiful princess in all the world?

LUCY: Yes, your highness.

PRINCESS: I have blonde hair.

LUCY: The only blonde hair in the kingdom.

PRINCESS: Aren't I lucky?

LUCY: Well, you banished every other blonde — or forced them to dye their hair...purple. You fired any maid you thought was prettier than you. You made —

PRINCESS: Yes, well all that's not important now. The important thing is that I am the fairest in the land. Even the mirror says so.

LUCY: Does it?

PRINCESS: Well, it would if it could talk. It certainly shows me how pretty I am.

LUCY: You spend enough time looking at it.

PRINCESS: It's a shame that I have to marry some horrid prince I've never even met.

LUCY: They say he's very handsome.

PRINCESS: Handsome...pah!

LUCY: I think you're lucky, your highness. Prince Valiant...he sounds so dashing. He'll ride up on his mighty steed and sweep you off your feet. The handsome prince.

PRINCESS: But I deserve more than just a pretty-boy! I want a prince who's...who's kind.

LUCY: You're not kind.

PRINCESS: Who likes animals.

LUCY: But you don't like animals.

PRINCESS: Who's modest.

LUCY: But you'd have nothing in common!

PRINCESS: I'm sorry...were you talking? I wasn't paying any attention. Millie?

LUCY: Lucy, your highness.

PRINCESS: Whatever. What do peasants do about getting married? Do you get married?

LUCY: Of course. But we usually marry for love, not money.

PRINCESS: Well duh—you don't have any money. But at least you don't have to choose between a Prince you don't like or a frog.

LUCY: A frog?

PRINCESS: The jester told me that was my only option.

LUCY: I don't think you should take advice from a fool.

PRINCESS: Well, in all the story books, the fool turns out to be clever, and makes everything work out in the end.

LUCY: Not this fool. She's the worst fool ever.

PRINCESS: Then who can help me?

LUCY: Well, you could...

PRINCESS: What?

LUCY: Nothing.

PRINCESS: What?

LUCY: I shouldn't have mentioned...

PRINCESS: You didn't mention. You're going to mention now.

LUCY: Your highness!

PRINCESS: Stop it! See this? Tiara. I'm the princess here. Now — out with it!

LUCY: Well...You could ask the witch.

PRINCESS: Which witch?

LUCY: Wakenda Watt. Watt the Witch.

PRINCESS: What witch?

LUCY: Yes.

PRINCESS: What?

LUCY: Yes.

PRINCESS: Which witch?

LUCY: Watt.

PRINCESS: What?

LUCY: Exactly!

(*Beat.*)

PRINCESS: I have no idea what you're talking about!

LUCY: The witch.

PRINCESS: I want to know her name.

LUCY: Watt.

PRINCESS: The witch's name.

LUCY: Watt.

PRINCESS: I want you to tell me her name!

LUCY: I just told you her name.

PRINCESS: What is it?!

LUCY: Exactly!

PRINCESS: Her name is exactly?

LUCY: No, your highness, that would be silly. Her name is Watt.

PRINCESS: I'm asking you! *(Beat.)* What is the witch's name?

LUCY: Yes.

PRINCESS: She's called yes?

LUCY: No.

PRINCESS: So she's called what?

LUCY: Yes.

PRINCESS: If I asked you the witch's name, you would tell me what?

LUCY: Exactly!

(Beat.)

PRINCESS: If you say "exactly" one more time...I'm going to have your head cut off.

LUCY: Your highness!

PRINCESS: Just tell me — simply — the name of the witch.

LUCY: Watt.

PRINCESS: Tell me the name of the witch.

LUCY: Watt!

PRINCESS: TELL ME HER NAME!

LUCY: WATT IS HER NAME!

PRINCESS: *(A la Lou Costello:)* Whaddaya askin' me for?

LUCY: I'm telling you!

PRINCESS: You're telling me what?!

LUCY: EXCA...and bacon.

PRINCESS: Watch yourself.

LUCY: I'm sorry, your highness. Watt is a witch.

PRINCESS: A magical woman with a cauldron.

LUCY: That's her!   •

PRINCESS: Who?

LUCY: Watt.

PRINCESS: WHO?!

LUCY: You don't need to yell.

PRINCESS: I CAN YELL ALL I LIKE, I'M THE PRINCESS! *(Beat.)* Just tell me about this witch, and I don't care if her name is Abigail Smedgewick Chucklebottom!

LUCY: She's a scary old woman that lives in the forest in a little hovel. Everyone says she's a witch. I thought maybe she could help you.

PRINCESS: Yes! She could cast a spell on the prince and turn him into a frog! Wait, that wouldn't work, I'd still have to marry him.

LUCY: Well, if there's anyone that knows how to get you out of this, it's Watt the witch.

PRINCESS: Which what?

LUCY: Close enough.

PRINCESS: My father would never let me go into the forest.

LUCY: You can't always do what your father tells you.

PRINCESS: He's not just my father, he's the king.

LUCY: Even so...

PRINCESS: I have an idea!

LUCY: You do?

PRINCESS: I'll disguise myself...as a peasant! *(Searching the audience:)* I'll dress up in the nastiest, ugliest, poorest, smelliest, rottenest rags and tatters I can find. *(She notices Lucy again:)* Ooh! Give me your dress.

LUCY: What?

PRINCESS: We'll exchange clothes. I'll dress up as you and go see the witch. *(Beat.)* You can wear my dress.

(Lucy covets her dress...)

I'll be back within the hour.

(Lucy compares the size of the Princess' waistline to her own...)

LUCY: But, your Highness...

PRINCESS: Enough! I told you what was going to happen, and I'm the princess! Tiara! Now get to it!

LUCY: Yes, your highness.

(Lights fade as they start to undress.)

SCENE 3—THE PALACE

(The King and Queen are standing, center. The Fool enters.)

FOOL: Milord and lady!

KING: Yes?

FOOL: May I present his royal highness...the Prince Valiant!

(PRINCE VALIANT enters—and strikes a pose at the doorway. The King and Queen do not notice him.)

QUEEN: That's not funny at all.

KING: It's silly. As if the Prince would turn up on the wrong day.

QUEEN: What kind of an idiot would he be, to turn up a day too early?

KING: Only a Prince with the brains of a mosquito—

QUEEN: A sick mosquito!

KING: A squashed mosquito!

QUEEN: A sick squashed mosquito!

FOOL: *(Aside to PRINCE:)* All squished and mooshy—yeuch!

KING: —would be so dumb, so ignorant, so FOOLISH as to turn up a day early.

(The King turns, and sees the Prince. Double take. Ah what the hey, triple take. [In the 2009 production, there was a seven-take. The king, the queen, the king and the queen, the jester, the king and the jester, the king and the queen and the jester, and finally all four of them!])

Agh!

QUEEN: Prince Valiant!

KING: Oh we were not expecting...

QUEEN: We were just...uh...

KING: We were just talking about—a different Prince.

QUEEN: *(Looking around for inspiration:)* Oh yes, Prince...Prince Chair. Door. Carpet!

KING: Good old Prince Carpet.

VALIANT: Prince Carpet?

QUEEN: Yes, a very old—

KING: Worn—

QUEEN: Family.

VALIANT: He sounds like a bit of a knucklehead. Glad I'm not as dumb as Prince Carpet.

FOOL: Of course. You're much smarter than a carpet.

VALIANT: *(To the Fool:)* Thank you. You must be the King.

FOOL: He's the King.

VALIANT: *(To the King:)* King Erroneous!

KING: Heironymous—

VALIANT: Heironymous! I am Prince Valiant. I have come to ask for your daughter's hand in marriage. Actually, all of her.

KING: Wonderful.

VALIANT: *(To the Fool:)* And you must be the Queen.

QUEEN: I am the queen! That's the Jester.

VALIANT: Oh, of course. Silly mistake, it must be the hat. So where is everyone? I was expecting to ride up on my shining white steed, and be surrounded by an adoring crowd for a royal wedding.

QUEEN: But the wedding's tomorrow.

VALIANT: Are you sure?   I thought it was Christmas tomorrow.

QUEEN: It's both.

VALIANT: A Christmas wedding?   How confusing.   We won't know which presents are for the wedding and which ones are for Christmas.

KING: Well...there may not be very many presents.

QUEEN: We hate to say it — but we're poor.

VALIANT: Poor?!   You live in a palace!   *(He looks at it:)* A very small, rather run down palace.

KING: We used to be rich.   But the royal treasury was robbed.

VALIANT: Robbed?   You mean, changing the furniture and painting the walls?

KING: No, that's *redecorated*.   Robbed is when things get stolen.

VALIANT: Oh, *robbed*.   Well, that's terrible.   What color is it? *(Reaction:)* I mean, what did they take?

KING: Everything.

QUEEN: My jewels!

KING: My gold!

FOOL: My string!

   (Everyone looks at her.)

I collect string...what?

VALIANT: So your wealth has been stolen.

KING: Yes.

VALIANT: No presents.

QUEEN: No.

VALIANT: Well...that's okay. Once I marry your daughter, we'll go and live in my palace, which has gold floors.

KING: Gold floors!

VALIANT: Gold ceilings.

QUEEN: Gold ceilings!

VALIANT: Gold windows.

FOOL: Gold wind—How'd you see through them?

VALIANT: I leave them open. I'm so rich, I have the outside air conditioned!

KING AND QUEEN: Oooh!

VALIANT: Now show me to the Princess!

FOOL: This way, Moneybags. I mean, your richness.

(The Fool and the Prince exit.)

KING: We will be rich again, my dear.

QUEEN: Nothing must go wrong with the wedding.

KING: Nothing will go wrong, my dear.

QUEEN: Our daughter better like him.

KING: She doesn't have a choice. Not many princes around. Anyway, what's wrong with him? Perfectly fine prince...

QUEEN: Well, he doesn't seem too bright—

KING: No. If you gave him a penny for his thoughts, he'd owe you change — but he is better than a frog.

QUEEN: A frog?

(They turn, and start leaving together, talking as they go.)

KING: Yes. The jester was explaining to me just the other day the advantages of having a son-in-law whose legs are considered a delicacy...

(Lights out slowly.)

SCENE 4—THE FOREST

(Dark and gloomy. The scariest trees possible. The Princess, dressed in the Maid's outfit, creeps through the forest.)

PRINCESS: Oh my...it is dark and gloomy in a forest. I didn't think there'd be this many trees. Once you put them all together like this...it's so hard to see anything! The ground needs a good sweeping too—there's dirt all over it. There's no organization. It's not a bit like the royal gardens.

(She doesn't see ALLAN, a handsome young fellow gathering wood, until he speaks.)

ALLAN: The royal gardens?

PRINCESS: Eeek!

ALLAN: And when did you see the royal gardens, Miss? No, no...don't be alarmed, young lass. It's just me, the blacksmith's son.

PRINCESS: What are you doing creeping around in the forest?

ALLAN: I'm not the one creeping around. I'm cutting wood for my father.

PRINCESS: The blacksmith? Why does someone that works with iron need wood?

ALLAN: Why, for the forge, lassy. You burn the wood to heat the forge to heat the iron. Have you never seen a blacksmith at work? My father's the finest smith in the land. He once shoed a pony for the Princess herself.

PRINCESS: Oh...the princess? The fair, beautiful blonde Princess?

ALLAN: Princess Stuck-up, they call her. Or Princess Snooty-pants.

PRINCESS: What?!

ALLAN: The vainest woman in the kingdom. They say she's so shallow, she could drown on a wet sidewalk.

PRINCESS: Well, what nerve!

ALLAN: You should be careful, though. If she ever saw you, she would have you thrown into the dungeon for being so beautiful.

PRINCESS: Yes, I am. I mean, I certainly would. I mean...Smithy-boy—

ALLAN: Allan.

PRINCESS: Allan...where is the witch that lives in these woods?

ALLAN: A witch?

PRINCESS: Yes. Her name is Exactly. Maybe.

ALLAN: Exactly maybe?

PRINCESS: Maybe.

ALLAN: Exactly what?

PRINCESS: Don't start!

ALLAN: There's an old woman that lives in a hovel, further up the path.

PRINCESS: That's her!

ALLAN: Her name is Watt. Wakenda Watt.

PRINCESS: *(Realization:)* Oh. *(To the audience:)* You know, you could've just told me.

ALLAN: Just keep on going up the path. When you get to the deepest, darkest part of the forest—there's a little hut. That's hers.

PRINCESS: The forest gets darker than this?

ALLAN: Aye, lass. And if you don't hurry, you'll not reach her hut before nightfall.

PRINCESS: Oh my. Maybe I should go back...but I've come so far.

ALLAN: I could walk with you, if you'd like.

PRINCESS: Very well. I will allow you. And as we walk, you may tell me how pretty I am.

(As they start walking through the forest:)

ALLAN: Streuth, you must be almost as vain as the Princess herself!

PRINCESS: I am not vain!

ALLAN: Ah, vanity, thy name is...what is your name?

PRINCESS: It's Prince—Uh...Priscilla. Priscilla Peasant.

ALLAN: Pleased to meet you, Priscilla. I'm Allan. Allan, Allan the blacksmith's son. Works from dawn 'til day is done...

PRINCESS: That sounds like a poem.

ALLAN: Aye, a piece of one. An old, old poem. I was named after it... Then again, my father was Allan, and my grandfather before him. We're all born the son of a smith, and grow up to be blacksmiths and have sons of our own.

PRINCESS: And you like working as a smith?

ALLAN: I like shoeing the horses. You have to be very gentle with them, or they get frightened.

PRINCESS: Oh. Are you married?

ALLAN: Not yet, Priscilla. And you?

PRINCESS: Not if I can help it. That's why I'm going to see the witch.

ALLAN: I wouldn't call her witch. Not to her face, anyway.

PRINCESS: Is she a wicked witch?

ALLAN: You'll find out. That's her hut, just up there. Good luck, sweet Priscilla.

PRINCESS: You're not staying?

ALLAN: I have wood to gather. Mistress Watt will see you safe out of the forest, if you ask her right.

PRINCESS: Good bye.

ALLAN: 'Til we meet again.

(He leaves. The Princess goes to the hovel, as she is about to knock — the WITCH appears. This can be as simple as the actress emerging from the hovel, or a full on dance sequence with the WOODLAND SPRITES dancing around her as she prepares a bubbling cauldron.)

WAKENDA: The Princess fair. What brings you to my humble abode?

PRINCESS: How did you know I was here?

WAKENDA: Guess.

PRINCESS: Guess?

WAKENDA: Guess.

PRINCESS: You used a crystal ball to spy on me.

WAKENDA: No.

PRINCESS: You foretold my arrival in your cauldron of bubbling witchbrew.

WAKENDA: This is gumbo.

PRINCESS: Gumbo?

WAKENDA: Gumbo. Shrimp, sausages, potatoes. I'm very proud of my
gumbo.

PRINCESS: I don't care.

WAKENDA: It's not witchbrew. You don't make witchbrew with sausage, witchbrew is made with newt's eyes and fenney snake. Are you saying my cooking smells like fenney snake?

PRINCESS: No!

WAKENDA: Well, your answer is: No. I did not foretell your arrival in my cauldron of delicious homemade, extra spicy shrimp gumbo with yummy sausages. Make your last guess, or go back to the palace and quit wasting my time.

PRINCESS: Well...I don't know! You're a nosy old baggage, and you heard us talking!

WAKENDA: Exactly. Two lovebirds, trilling their song right past my hut — I'd have to have been deaf.

PRINCESS: But how did you know I was the princess?

WAKENDA: Well, young men with a fancy in their eye may not always see clearly, but your shoes aren't made for walking. Those soft hands have never scrubbed a floor or washed a dish — and your dress has creases that were made by someone a little...taller than you. I notice things. Plus, I've seen your face on silver coins.

PRINCESS: That's not really magic. Can you help me?

WAKENDA: What is it you need? A love potion?

PRINCESS: Tomorrow, I must wed a Prince I've never met. I want you to stop it. I don't want to marry him!

WAKENDA: If you've never met him, how do you know you don't want to marry him? Maybe you'll fall in love with him at first sight.

PRINCESS: I'd sooner marry the blacksmith's son!

WAKENDA: You could do worse—mayhap you should've looked at him a little closer...what's wrong with this Prince?

PRINCESS: He's rich and stupid.

WAKENDA: Sounds like a match.

PRINCESS: I'm not stupid! I may be vain, but—

WAKENDA: You admit it?

PRINCESS: Well, why shouldn't I be! I'm pretty. I'm a princess! My whole life, I've been told I'm the beautiful princess, I've been dressed up and put on display, I've been told what to wear and where I can go, and who I must marry. A dumb prince or a frog! That's my choice!

WAKENDA: Hey! I married a frog once. *(Beat.)* They're over-rated.

PRINCESS: I command you to stop the wedding!

WAKENDA: You command me? In my forest, you command me?

(Wakenda waves her hand—THUNDER ROLLS, Lights go darker. Dancing WOODLAND SPRITES emerge, and whirl round the Princess pulling her hair and plucking at her dress. The Princess cowers.)

(Wakenda waves the Sprites away.)

Now you've had a chance to think about it, I bet you wish you'd asked that differently.

PRINCESS: Mistress Watt, if you would be so good as to help me, I would be very grateful.

WAKENDA: That's much better. If you want to stop the wedding, you must give three gifts.

PRINCESS: Gifts?

WAKENDA: Tomorrow's Christmas, isn't it?

PRINCESS: Yes, but princesses don't give gifts, they get them. Lots of them. Last year, I got two ponies, so that if one broke, I could play with the other.

WAKENDA: Oy vey. Tomorrow, you must give three gifts. To your father, you must give a single hair from the crescent moon of the Crescent Moon Bear. To your mother, you must give a tear from the Dragon's eye. And to the man that you will marry, you must give a petal from the blood rose.

PRINCESS: But I don't want to marry him.

WAKENDA: Then don't give it to him. Give it to the one you do want to marry.

PRINCESS: Where will I find the Crescent Moon Bear? Or a dragon? Or the blood rose?

WAKENDA: If you go deeper into the forest, far past my —

PRINCESS: Hovel.

WAKENDA: House! ...across the dead stream and through the barren rocks, to the very deepest, darkest part of the forest —

PRINCESS: Oh my.

WAKENDA: As far as the other side of night—you will find a dark cave. That is where the Crescent Moon Bear lives. He will call the dragon.

PRINCESS: How does he get cell phone reception out there?

WAKENDA: When you pluck out one of the hairs from the crescent moon shape on his chest, he will cry out so loudly, the dragon will come to his aid.

PRINCESS: Oh.

WAKENDA: I didn't say this would be easy. The bear has sharp claws and big teeth.

PRINCESS: And then he calls a dragon?

WAKENDA: A dragon with sharper claws and bigger teeth. A bear can only eat you up. The dragon can burn you to a little pile of ash that will blow away in the wind.

PRINCESS: It's impossible!

WAKENDA: Well then, go ahead and marry your stupid prince. It's the easy way out.

PRINCESS: Never.

WAKENDA: Then you know what you have to do. Start walking.

PRINCESS: What about the blood rose?

WAKENDA: You'll find that when the time is right. It's getting later by the minute—and you have a long way to go.

PRINCESS: Thank you.

WAKENDA: Do you want some gumbo to take with you? It's got yummy sausages in it.

PRINCESS: No thanks. I'm good.

WAKENDA: Oh, take some. Here. You'll appreciate some nice warm gumbo on your journey. The night will be as cold as a cruel word, and the wind as sharp as an icicle.

(She hands the princess a miniature cauldron.)

And here—this will hold a dragon's tear.

(She hands the Princess a crystal vial on a chain, which the Princess puts on as a necklace.)

Good luck. You have a long way to go, and it's uphill all the way...and all the way back.

PRINCESS: But it's getting dark...

WAKENDA: You're right, I should've said it's uphill and dark all the way.

(She goes back into her hut, cackling.)

(The Princess looks back the way she came in...but decides to go on, and exits on the far side of the stage. Blackout.)

SCENE 5 — THE PRINCESS' CHAMBERS

(Lucy, dressed as the princess, sits at her table, brushing her hair.)

LUCY: One, two, three...

(She shrugs, and puts the brush down. With a furtive glance, she tries on the tiara and admires herself.)

(The Prince enters.)

VALIANT: Princess?

LUCY: Oh!

VALIANT: I am...

(They look at each other. Love at first sight. True love.)

...Prince Valiant. You're more beautiful than everyone says.

LUCY: You're the handsome Prince!

VALIANT: Yes. And tomorrow, I shall be your handsome husband.

LUCY: Oh dear. I'm not...

VALIANT: Don't tell me you're having second thoughts.

(He kneels in front of her.)

I couldn't stand it. You are the woman I have dreamed of my whole life.

LUCY: Wow...You have incredible eyes.

VALIANT: Two of them.

LUCY: Wow.

VALIANT: Princess?

LUCY: Oh.

VALIANT: I know I may not be very clever—in the third grade, the other kids teased me because they could do long division and fractions, and I was twenty-two...but I will be a good husband, and kind and true to you.

LUCY: I'm not...I can't marry a prince. I'm poor.

VALIANT: I know, your father told me. It doesn't matter. I would marry you if you were a scullery maid.

LUCY: Or a ladies' maid?

VALIANT: I would marry you if you scrubbed the toilets at Dodger Stadium. I just wouldn't kiss your hand.

(He kisses her hand. Her arm. As he works his way up, the Fool enters.)

FOOL: Your highness!

(The Prince leaps up, the Maid squeaks in alarm.)

VALIANT: I was just kissing her hand!

FOOL: You!

VALIANT: Yes me. Her hand, was kissing. *(Correcting himself:)* I.

LUCY: I must go!

VALIANT: No, don't leave!

(She runs out of the room.)

(To the Fool:) You better not have ruined this! *(After the maid:)* Wait! My love!

(The Prince runs after her.)

FOOL: Oh dear. Oh my deary, deary me. The prince and the maid! What was she doing, dressed up like the princess? Where is the princess! I must run and tell the King!

(She gets to the door, and turns back.)

The King...the King that has already threatened me with the dungeon once this evening. If I tell him his future son-in-law has got his eye on the maid—he'll be furious! He'll take it out on me, I know he will!

KING (O.S.): Jester!

FOOL: I must hide!

(She desperately looks around, tries hiding behind a picture or under a handkerchief.)

KING (O.S.): Jester, where are you?

FOOL: Hide me!

(She runs into the audience, clambering over people, and ducks down behind some seats, or throws someone's coat over her head... The King enters.)

KING: Sweetie, have you seen the Jester? Ah, not here. *(To Audience:)* What is going on out there? Have you seen the Jester?

FOOL: Tell him I'm not here!

KING: Who said that?

FOOL: The little girl in the front row! With the terrible jokes!

KING: You don't sound like her at all.

FOOL: *(Falsetto:)* I have a cold.

(The King looks at the little girl closely.)

KING: Say that again.

FOOL: I'm not here!

KING: Amazing. Your lips didn't even move.

FOOL: Botox!

(The King sees the Jester.)

KING: Jester! Stop fooling around!

FOOL: That's what you pay me to do.

KING: Where's the Princess? Have you seen the Prince?

FOOL: Oh, the Prince was just here, he went for a moonlight stroll with the mai—mai—maybe he wasn't here.

KING: Was he here or not?

FOOL: He was here, he was kissing the mai—mai—mainly he was kissing her. Kissing her hand...and—and then they went out in the royal gardens.

KING: Well, it sounds like they're getting along splendidly. Now come with me, I need your help with the Christmas tree wedding cake for tomorrow.

FOOL: Christmas tree wedding cake?

KING: It's a Christmas wedding. What else would one have? Anyway, I need someone to hold the tree steady while I put the icing on.

FOOL: Where's the cook?

KING: When I told her about the tree cake, she yelled at me for two minutes, and then left in a huff.

FOOL: *(A la Groucho Marx:)* I don't blame her. I'd leave in a minute and a huff.

(The King grabs her ear and drags her out.)

KING: You're still not funny.

FOOL: No, Sire.

(Exeunt. Lights out.)

SCENE 6 — THE PALACE

(A lighting shift — late at night.   Torchlight flickers on the walls — or a moon rises in the background. Prince Valiant and Lucy are strolling hand in hand.)

VALIANT: Your cheeks are as soft as a marshmallow. Your eyes — they're all swirly, like spoiled milk poured into blue coffee.

LUCY: No one's ever said such nice things to me. Prince Valiant?

VALIANT: Yes?

LUCY: Kiss me. Kiss me like the morning dew kisses a flower petal.

VALIANT: All wet and drippy?

LUCY: Okay.

(He leans into her. Just as they are about to kiss, the Fool runs on.)

FOOL: There you are!

VALIANT: Ah! I was just...She had something in her eye. I was just going to get it out.

FOOL: With your lips?

VALIANT: Well...

FOOL: What if the King sees you!

VALIANT: Oh dear...My love — I'll see you soon.   In the morning, we wed!

(He leaves.)

FOOL: You'll wed? The prince and the maid? What is going on!

LUCY: Oh, Jester — the most wonderful thing. And the most terrible thing.

FOOL: Which is which?

LUCY: They're both the same thing.

FOOL: *(A la Gary Coleman:)* What'choo talking 'bout, Lucy?

LUCY: The Princess made me dress in her clothes — and the Prince has fallen in love with me!

FOOL: I figured that much, if I hadn't come in when I did, this might not've been a family show!

LUCY: You don't understand — I love him too. I've fallen for him utterly and completely. It's the most wonderful thing ever.

FOOL: *(Realizing:)* He doesn't even know who you are! He thinks you're the princess!

LUCY: I know. That's the terrible part. How can I tell him?

FOOL: I think he'll notice when he sees a different woman at his wedding tomorrow. Maybe not, with this one.

LUCY: What can I do?

FOOL: There's nothing you can do — he's a Prince! He must marry a Princess — not a lady's maid, no matter how good she looks in a dress.

LUCY: You like my dress?

FOOL: It's not yours, it's the Princess'! ...Where is the Princess?

LUCY: She went to the forest to see the witch.

FOOL: She WHAT?! Why would she do such a thing?

LUCY: I told her to. Was that wrong?

FOOL: It's the middle of the night! She's not back yet—she could be lost in the forest, or have been eaten by wild animals.

LUCY: I'm sure she made it safely to the witch's house.

FOOL: That's not comforting!

LUCY: What can we do? I love Prince Valiant. Don't tell the King.

FOOL: The King is asleep. In the morning, he will wake, and then everything will fall to pieces. The Princess out all night, the maid and the prince...and you know the worst part?

LUCY: What?

FOOL: I will get all of the blame! I always do..

LUCY: I don't blame you.

FOOL: Yes, but you're not the one that will have me thrown in a dungeon!

LUCY: I'm sure she'll be back in the morning.

FOOL: And you will have to tell the Prince the truth. Tomorrow, he weds another.

LUCY: Oh, Jester...I'm so unhappy!

FOOL: I could tell you a joke.

(She looks at the Jester — and bursts into tears. Blackout.)

SCENE 7 — THE FOREST — BY THE BEAR'S CAVE

(Wind. Snow. Lightning flickers across the stage, revealing a gaping cave. A low, rumbling SNORING SOUND from within.)

(The Princess staggers onto the stage, blown by the wind, frozen. She puts the gumbo down, and slowly approaches the cave.)

PRINCESS: Mister Bear? ...Mister Bear?

(The CRESCENT MOON BEAR leaps out, ROARING!)

(She SCREAMS and runs back.)

BEAR: WHO DISTURBS ME!

PRINCESS: It's Princess Stuck-up! I mean...I'm...the Princess. Please don't eat me!

BEAR: I was hibernating!

PRINCESS: I need your help.

BEAR: HELP?!? You dare ask me for my help?

PRINCESS: Mister Bear — I'm the Princess. My father is a very, very important — he's the King. He sent me here to command you...Ooh! Look, it's the North star!

(As the Bear looks, she hesitantly reaches out for his chest.)

(The Bear catches her hand.)

BEAR: You're trying to steal a hair from my chest!

PRINCESS: How did you — I mean, no. Why would I ever...well...not at all.

BEAR: People hunt unicorns for their spiral horns and tigerlopes for their stripey antlers...and every time I lie down for a winter's sleep, someone tries to pluck a hair from the crescent moon on my chest. Begone! Or I shall eat you up!

(He ROARS again — she scurries back.)

(The Bear goes back into his cave.)

PRINCESS: Oh no. I've come all this way, and I'm so cold...I can't give up now.

(She turns, goes back to the cave and pounds on the entrance.)

Please Mister Bear, I crossed the dead stream and climbed the barren rocks and walked all this way in the snow. Won't you take pity on me? I'm freezing. And I'm blonde. And I'm pretty! Do you really want to be the bear that said no to a Princess?

(The Bear reappears.)

BEAR: REOWR! I've eaten the last three, and I'm still hungry! Run away or you'll be next!

(He goes into the cave.)

(The Princess starts walking away.)

PRINCESS: I knew this was impossible. I can't pluck a hair off an angry bear! And then a dragon will come? I should never have come out here. I guess I'll have to marry the stupid prince.

(She sits down.)

(To Audience — improv to reactions:) Do you think I should go home and marry the stupid Prince? ...Should I try one more time? ...What if he eats me up? He's so hungry! ...What? I could give him the what? ...The gumbo? ...You're right!

(She picks up the gumbo, and goes back to the cave.)

Mister Bear! Mister Bear! I'm not frightened, you hear me?!

BEAR: REOWR...What? Run away.

PRINCESS: No.

BEAR: You have to.

PRINCESS: I won't. If you're going to eat me up, you better start, but I'm not going to be frightened away, no matter how much you roar.

BEAR: Really?

PRINCESS: Definitely.

BEAR: What if I gnash my teeth? ...No? Swipe at you?

PRINCESS: I have no choice. But if you're hungry, I will give you my gumbo. Mistress Watt made it. She was the one that said if I didn't steal one of your hairs, I would have to marry the stupid Prince.

BEAR: You have gumbo?

PRINCESS: It has yummy sausages in it.

(She gives him the gumbo.)

BEAR: My favorite!

(He sits down and pulls out a spoon.)

(He pats the ground next to him. The Princess joins him – he offers her a taste.)

BEAR: I don't really eat people. I just say that, because all I want to do is sleep. No one leaves me alone.

PRINCESS: I just need one hair. Then I'll let you be.

BEAR: It hurts. I always cry.

PRINCESS: And then the dragon will come.

BEAR: You know about the dragon? That's good, it comes as quite a shock to most people. Well...okay. Get it over with.

PRINCESS: Thank you, Mister Bear.

(She reaches out, and plucks a hair from the crescent moon shape on his chest.)

BEAR: *(Howling:)* AH-WOOOOOOOOH! Ow, ow,ow! That stings!

PRINCESS: Thank you.

BEAR: Now the dragon will come! You better run away, or she'll eat you up!

PRINCESS: I can't—I need a tear from it—her.

BEAR: A dragon's tear? You'll never get a tear from the dragon.

PRINCESS: I have to. I have to give a dragon's tear to my mother, or she'll make me marry someone I don't love.

BEAR: Don't you know? A dragon only cries once in a thousand years.

PRINCESS: Once in a thousand years?! Then how will I ever get a tear?

BEAR: That's a big problem. Although, it's been a long time since she cried. Maybe it's been a thousand years, maybe not. Maybe only eight hundred, I forget. You might have to wait a couple of hundred years.

PRINCESS: I can't do that!

(Thumping footsteps approach.)

BEAR: She's coming!

(The Bear runs back...but returns, to the Princess' relief.)

(He picks up the gumbo and runs back to his cave.)

(He returns.)

(To the audience:) Hide!

(The Bear runs back into his cave – the Princess cowers behind a tree.)

(The footsteps get louder...)

(The DRAGON emerges – huge and terrifying.)

DRAGON: Who has awoken me from my great sleep!

PRINCESS: It was the bear! It wasn't me!

DRAGON: The bear stays quiet unless he is disturbed! Who has stolen one of his hairs?

PRINCESS: That was—that was me.

DRAGON: Then prepare to be eaten up!

PRINCESS: No, please! I need one of your tears!

DRAGON: A tear? I have not cried in...in ages.

PRINCESS: So you should be due, right?

DRAGON: I am not sad.

PRINCESS: Tomorrow, I have to wed someone I don't love. Isn't that sad?

DRAGON: Not for me. La la la la-la la.

(The Dragon does a little happy dance.)

PRINCESS: Isn't there anything you can think of that's sad? Puppies lost in the woods? Getting socks for Christmas? Transformers Two?! *

DRAGON: The last time I cried was eight hundred and twenty-six years ago. My husband forgot our anniversary.

PRINCESS: Oh, that's terrible!

DRAGON: It certainly was for him, I gobbled him up on the spot.

PRINCESS: But that means you won't cry for another one hundred and seventy-four years!

DRAGON: You are good at math.

PRINCESS: Not that anyone cares. They just want me to look pretty.

DRAGON: That is a bit sad. What is seventy-two times one hundred and three?

PRINCESS: Seven thousand four hundred and sixteen.

DRAGON: Right! Ask me one.

PRINCESS: Promise you won't eat me up?

DRAGON: Well...I will give you three tries. If you can ask me a question I cannot answer, then I will not eat you.

PRINCESS: Ok. What's sixteen million three hundred thousand and three divided by seven?

DRAGON: Two million, three hundred and twenty-eight thousand, five hundred and seventy-two. I went to school for twelve hundred years, you know. I learned a lot of math.

PRINCESS: Oh. Well...Who was the King of Thrain in the Year of the Emancipation of Weasels?

DRAGON: The King of Thrain?

PRINCESS: You didn't say it had to be a math question, you just said three questions.

DRAGON: The King of Thrain, in the Year of the Emancipation of Weasels...hmmm...

PRINCESS: You don't know, do you?

DRAGON: King Henry the Two Thirds. I met him once. He tasted like chicken, and I got a piece of his armor stuck in my teeth for two weeks.

PRINCESS: Oh dear. You know everything, don't you?

DRAGON: I have been around a lot longer than you, honey.

PRINCESS: Well—I don't...

DRAGON: Ask your last question. I am getting hungry.

PRINCESS: Ah—What is it that a man stands up to do, a woman sits down to do, and a dog lifts one leg to do?

DRAGON: WHAT?!

PRINCESS: I overheard it from the Jester.

DRAGON: I can't answer that! There are kids watching!

PRINCESS: Well, if you can't answer it, you can't eat me up.

DRAGON: Well, that is...you cannot answer it either!

PRINCESS: Yes I can. They shake hands. *(Standing:)* I'm Mr. Heironymous Bosch, pleased to meet you. *(Miming sitting and presenting her hand:)* Lady Magnolia Cherryblossom, charmed, I'm sure.

(On all fours, pants, woofs, and raises a forepaw.)

(The Dragon laughs...and laughs and LAUGHS!)

DRAGON: They shake hands! Oh, that is so funny! ...I have not laughed so much since I ate an official that came to tell me I was an endangered species! They shake hands! Hee hee hee! Oh, I am laughing so hard, I am crying!

PRINCESS: You're laughing so hard you're crying? You have tears in your eyes?

DRAGON: Ha ha! Hee hee hee!

PRINCESS: Can I have one?

DRAGON: Sure, honey...they shake hands!

(The Princess holds her vial up to the dragon's eye.)

PRINCESS: I have it! The tear of a dragon! Now, I won't have to marry that stupid prince!

(Lights out.)

SCENE 8 — THE FOREST

(The lights come up slowly — sunrise in the forest. The Woodland Sprites dance around the Princess — she might wake and dreamily dance with them. When the dance is over, the Princess is again asleep on the ground. Allan enters.)

ALLAN: Good morning, Priscilla!

(She wakes up.)

PRINCESS: Huh? Who?

ALLAN: Good morning, lass. You slept the night in the forest?

PRINCESS: I climbed over the barren rocks, and past the dead stream...but it was too dark to find my way through all the trees. And I was so tired.

ALLAN: You went beyond the barren rocks last night? But there's terrible creatures out there!

PRINCESS: Yes, the Crescent Moon Bear — but he's not as bad as everyone says.

ALLAN: He eats people!

PRINCESS: No he doesn't...he's just grumpy when he gets woken up.

ALLAN: Why did you go so far?

PRINCESS: I had to get something. A gift for my parents, so that they won't make me marry someone I do not love.

ALLAN: You spoke to Mistress Watt yesterday...this sounds like her doing.

PRINCESS: Yes, it was.

ALLAN: Here — let me help you up. Oh, you're all covered in mud. And you have leaves in your hair.

PRINCESS: That's okay. I'll brush them out later.

ALLAN: Really? Yesterday...you seemed different.

PRINCESS: Maybe I was, a little. I think...I don't know. I was almost eaten by a dragon. It just seems a little silly to worry about a leaf in my hair.

ALLAN: There's a spider on it.

PRINCESS: *(Leaping up and down:)* Agh! Get it off! Get it off!

ALLAN: I'm joking! I'm joking!

(She playfully smacks him. Smiles.)

PRINCESS: You're so funny. Watch out for that snake.

ALLAN: *(Jumping onto the princess' back:)* WAAAH!

PRINCESS: I'm joking!

(They laugh together.)

I have to get to the Palace. I have something to give to my parents.

ALLAN: Do you work there?

PRINCESS: Kind of.

ALLAN: If you're passing through the woods sometime...

PRINCESS: Maybe. Or the next time my pony needs shoeing.

ALLAN: A pony! A maid with her own pony!

PRINCESS: Yeah, keep laughing, smithy-boy. We'll see. Bye.

ALLAN: Bye!

(She runs off – looking back to make sure he's watching her go – which he is, of course.)

SCENE 9—THE PALACE.

(The Jester rushes about, hanging various Christmas decorations about the palace. This might also be a transformative dance number, with the dancers decorating while the Jester gets in the way as she tries to help.)

(When the madness is over and the castle decorated, the Prince and Lucy enter, canoodling.)

VALIANT: Oh, my darling.

LUCY: Oh, my sweet Prince.

VALIANT: Just think—in a few hours we shall be wed.

LUCY: There's...there's something I have to tell you.

VALIANT: Really? Because I have something to confess as well.

LUCY: You first.

VALIANT: Maybe you should go first.

(The Fool enters.)

FOOL: You two! Still? Hide! The King and Queen are coming!

LUCY: Right now?

(The King enters with the Queen.)

FOOL: Yes, right now! Quick, hide in the audience! No, wait, under a—behind a—under here!

(She's trying to duck under the Queen's skirts...realizes.)

Your highness! I was just...

QUEEN: Being foolish. We are not amused.

FOOL: Sorry.

KING: Merry Christmas! What a perfect morning for a Christmas Wedding! And there's the two lovebirds...LUCY!

LUCY: Eeek!

FOOL: *(A la Ricky Ricardo:)* You got some 'splainin' to do, Lucy!

(The King shoots a look at the Jester, but his attention returns to Lucy immediately.)

KING: What are you doing with the prince!

VALIANT: Sire, I love her. We spent the whole night just walking, and talking. I am deeply in love with her.

KING: No!

QUEEN: You can't marry her!

VALIANT: So...you know?

KING: Of course! D'you think we don't know our own maid!

VALIANT: The maid?

QUEEN: Why are you canoodling with the maid?

VALIANT: I was with the Princess!

QUEEN: That's not the Princess!

KING: That's the maid, you mosquito-brained idiot!

LUCY: I'm...I'm so sorry, Prince Valiant...I wanted to tell you.

VALIANT: You're not the Princess.

LUCY: No. I'm so sorry.

VALIANT: But that means I have to marry...

(The Princess enters, carrying her gifts.)

PRINCESS: Me! I am the princess.

VALIANT: Oh no! I mean, Milady.

(The Prince bows.)

KING: Lucy, you're fired. *(To the Fool:)* And you! This is all your fault...somehow.

FOOL: I knew it.

QUEEN: *(To the Princess:)* Come, child. Let the wedding begin!

PRINCESS: No! This has nothing to do with the Jester, Lucy is not fired, and I'm not marrying the Prince!

FOOL: What?

VALIANT & LUCY: WHAT?!

KING & QUEEN: WHAT?!

QUEEN: You most certainly are!

KING: We went to considerable trouble to arrange this!

PRINCESS: I have a gift for you.

(Pause.)

KING: For me?

PRINCESS: Yes. For everyone.

QUEEN: But you don't give gifts. You're a princess, you get them.

PRINCESS: This Christmas is different. I'm different. This is for you. And this is for you. *(She turns to the Fool:)* And...I know it's nothing special...but I wanted to give you this. Merry Christmas.

(She hands the Jester a box. The Jester reaches in and pulls out an immense ball of string.)

FOOL: Your highness! Thank you! I have string! I have string! Stringety-stringety-string!

(She capers off stage.)

(The King and Queen open their gift boxes.)

KING: Oh my...It's...a hair? A white hair. Am I going bald? Do I need hair?

QUEEN: It's a little vial. Oh! Perfume, of course. *(She opens it:)* Funny, it doesn't smell at all. *(She tastes it:)* Ew! It's all salty.

(The Queen empties the vial, and drops it in disgust.)

KING: I don't think I need another hair, I've got lots.

(He throws it away.)

Well, on with the wedding!

PRINCESS: No, wait! I'm not getting married!

KING: Yes, you are. You're a princess, and there aren't many princes around. This is the only one we could find for you, so marry him you shall. I am the King, and you will obey me.

QUEEN: We know what's best for you, believe us.

PRINCESS: But I crossed the dead stream and I climbed the barren rocks and I braved the bear and I beat the dragon, and I gave you the hair and the tear and everything!

QUEEN: She's babbling.

(Three LOUD KNOCKS come from the door. Everyone stops and turns.)

(Wakenda enters, carried piggyback style by Allan.)

WAKENDA: Blessings be upon this...palace. Thanks for helping me here, bear. My legs aren't what they used to be.

ALLAN: I don't know how much help I was—you carried me over the rough bits.

WAKENDA: I wanted you here.

QUEEN: Mistress Watt!

KING: What?

QUEEN: Yes.

KING: What did you call her?

QUEEN: Yes.

(The King looks confused—Wakenda interrupts.)

WAKENDA: Call me Wakenda—it will save a lot of dialogue.

KING: You know this woman?

QUEEN: She gave me a potion once to—uh...never mind, honey.

PRINCESS: *(Crying:)* Mistress Watt! It didn't work, it didn't work at all! I did everything you said. I got the hair from the Crescent Moon Bear, and I made the dragon laugh and caught its tear...and my parents threw them away and it's all gone wrong! Now I have to marry the stupid Prince!

(Wakenda goes to her.)

WAKENDA: Of course they threw them away. A hair? A drop of salty water? They were worthless.

PRINCESS: You are a wicked witch!

WAKENDA: I wouldn't call me a witch at all...although some call me a wise woman. Tell me, who climbed the barren rocks? Who crossed the dead stream, and walked as far as the other side of night?

PRINCESS: I did.

WAKENDA: Who was that?

PRINCESS: Princess...stuck-up. Princess snooty pants.

WAKENDA: Who came back?

PRINCESS: Well...

WAKENDA: You convinced the Crescent Moon Bear to give you a hair right from his own chest. Do you not think you can get your father to listen to you? You calmed the angry dragon, and made her laugh 'til she cried—can you not bring your own mother that happiness? The princess that came back from the forest is not the same as the one that walked into it. She is a princess worthy of a true prince.

PRINCESS: But I don't want to marry him.

VALIANT: She can't marry me anyway—he's the real prince.

(He's pointing at Allan.)

EVERYONE: WHAT?!

VALIANT: I met him in the forest. I was cutting wood—he said if I gave him my clothes, I could have a fine white horse and go and marry a stuck-up, snootypants Princess.

ALLAN: It's true. I didn't want to marry someone vain and shallow...so I traded my clothes and my horse...But I would marry you.

PRINCESS: You're the real prince?

LUCY: *(To Valiant:)* And you're just a woodcutter?

VALIANT: Actually, I'm the blacksmith's son.

LUCY: You're a blacksmith? That's so hot.

VALIANT: It does get pretty warm by that forge, true.

QUEEN: I'm confused.

WAKENDA: Your daughter is marrying the true prince. Prince Allan.

QUEEN: He's dressed as a peasant.

WAKENDA: So's your daughter. It's not the clothes, look at him for who he is.

PRINCESS: He's kind, and he likes animals...and he's modest.

ALLAN: Even in mud and leaves...you are beautiful where it matters — on the inside. So beautiful, any princess should surely throw you in a dungeon.

PRINCESS: I feel like I've escaped from a dungeon. If I knew where to find the blood rose, I'd give you a petal right now, and we would be married.

WAKENDA: Check your pockets.

(The Princess reaches into her pocket, and pulls out a crimson rose.)

PRINCESS: But how?

WAKENDA: You carried it with you all the time. You just couldn't find it until you found the true prince. ...Well, okay, so I might be a bit of a witch. You never know, with magic.

(The Princess hands Allan the rose.)

(Wakenda waves her hands magically.)

(They chastely kiss over the rose.)

(Prince Valiant dips Lucy upstage and kisses her.)

(The King and Queen embrace.)

KING: We shall have a double wedding — and a celebration that shall last a week. This is truly the best gift I have ever been given.

QUEEN: And the best Christmas ever.

(The Fool enters, staggering under a precariously carried Christmas tree decorated with a bride and groom at the top, and lavishly covered in whipped cream.)

FOOL: Sire! Milords, Ladies, and gentlemen! The Christmas tree Wedding Cake!

(She trips — falls backwards, the tree landing on top of her. She sits up, covered in cream.)

(Everyone looks at the King.)

(The King bursts into LAUGHTER!)

KING: Now, that's funny!

(They all LAUGH as music rises.)

(Lights out. End of play.)

The Author Speaks

What inspired you to write this play?
In 2005, I was part of the Coop Theatre Company in Los Angeles, which had just finished the run of a multi-year serial comedy. One actress, Christy Buchholz, had been scheduled to play a character called "The Christmas Princess," but the role was cut. She lamented to me that she'd always wanted to be a Christmas Princess and now she'd never get the chance...by the end of the year, this play was written and she was in the title role. Actors take note—complaining to playwrights sometimes pays off!

Was the structure of the play influenced by any other work?
It is definitely inspired by the British pantomimes I grew up watching—but tempered for American audiences. It also draws heavily on the classic fairytales—the original, primal stories that illuminate our shared human nature. The Crescent Moon Bear comes from a Japanese folk tale, and it's another story that hides some real depth.

Have you dealt with the same theme in other works that you have written?
The theme of a young woman finding the inner strength to come to terms with her parents on her own level does crop up in my other plays, notably the very heavy adult drama *Past Curfew*. That play doesn't have a dragon, though, or a pie in the face.

What writers have had the most profound effect on your style?
I love the way Edward Albee and Tracy Letts handle dysfunctional family relationships, and David Mamet's musical rhythm to his dialogue...but I'm still affected most by

the lessons learned from my high school creative writing teacher. You may have heard of him, he retired the year I graduated to write a book about his childhood in Ireland (*Angela's Ashes* by Frank McCourt).

What do you hope to achieve with this work?
While I wrote this play to make kids and their parents share some laughter, I'd like to think it might inspire people to realize that there really is true magic in the world—and it comes from inside ourselves.

What are the most common mistakes that occur in productions of your work?
I saw a rehearsal once where two actors had been struggling to find a moment. They knew it was there, but the scene wasn't working. After trying it a half dozen ways, the director suggested taking a long—and meaningful—pause before a key line. It worked. It was also in the script all along, described as "a deadly pause." Theatre is collaborative, you have to make it your own...but in a well-written play, everything is there for a reason. An ellipsis or a dash makes all the difference to the delivery of a line. The days when elaborate, detailed stage directions ("she crosses S.L") were added by the stage manager are long gone. In a modern play the stage directions are used sparingly, and added by the playwright only when necessary. The director that crosses them out does so at their peril. Know the punctuation conventions in playwriting, and try the line as it actually is first...it's usually right.

Are any characters modeled after real life or historical figures?
They are modeled after fairy-tale archetypes—who are of course modeled after aspects of each of us.

Shakespeare gave advice to the players in *Hamlet***; if you could give advice to your cast what would it be?**
In this particular play, there can be a tendency to play everything for a laugh. The laughs are there—particularly in the asides to the audience—but the characters have real emotional depth as well. Play them for real—you'll find that's where the real humor lies. After the show, stay and talk to the kids in the audience in character. They will love it—you will love it. At a couple of the productions I've seen of this play, after the curtain call, the cast brought the kids on stage and danced with them. You will make lifelong theatre lovers.

How was the first production different from the vision that you created in your mind?
The first production was done on a shoestring budget. The play worked, and I loved it, but I thought they needed a bigger, more elaborate dragon. It turned out I was quite wrong—they used a puppet dragon-head on a pole, with two fabric wings that stretched across the stage. When it came out of the darkness, the wings (held by a pair of dancers) reached out as though the dragon was about to engulf the entire audience...absolutely terrifying and wonderful. I think it cost about twenty bucks worth of materials they already had in the scene shop, but the effect was priceless.

About the Author

Arthur M. Jolly was recognized by the Academy of Motion Picture Arts and Sciences with a Nicholl Fellowship in Screenwriting in 2006 and works as a screenwriter and playwright in Los Angeles, represented by the Brant Rose Agency. His plays have won numerous awards, and been produced internationally. He was born in England, but also lived in Kenya, Madagascar and France until the age of 11, when his family moved to New York City. He attended Stuyvesant High School, where he cut his economics class to sit in on creative writing classes with Pulitzer Prize winner Frank McCourt—then an unknown English teacher. Arthur's early career was in the film industry in New York, where for 12 years he worked every possible below-the-line job, from stuntman and special effects artist to food stylist and cockroach wrangler. (Not the same production.) He has over 150 film and television credits, but some of them are cockroach wrangling. These days he will only admit to being a writer. More at www.arthurjolly.com.

More from YouthPLAYS

Secret Life Under the Stairs by Kris Knutsen
Young Audiences. 30-35 minutes. 2 males, 2 females.

Nothing much seems to happen in the isolated town of Echo, Nevada...that is until a new kid shows up and disturbs the secret hideout of a group of not-so-friendly misfits. LuLu, Bizzy, and twins Catch and Field spend an afternoon discovering things they never knew about friendship, trust, and a mysterious and disgusting "Death Jar." A play about making friends, navigating change, and exploring imaginative worlds that are often lurking under the stairs.

Producing a play? Visit the ultimate resource site for producers at all levels, packed with tips from top professionals:
www.ProduceaPlay.com

Un-Holy Nite by Samantha Macher
Comedy with music. 40-50 minutes. 7-13 males, 2-9 females (9-21 performers possible).

Five comic Christmas vignettes are themed around the (public domain) Christmas carol that accompanies them--perfect for the school that wants to do a showcase of both actors and singers for a holiday performance. The stories range from guys hanging out at a holiday sweater party waiting for girls to show up (***Jingle Belles***) to a story about a mysterious Christmas present waiting to be opened (***It Came Upon a Midnite Clear***). There's something in this series of holiday comedies for everyone.

Persephone Underground by Carol S. Lashof
Drama. 45-60 minutes. 2-15 males, 7-20+ females, 8-10 either (19-45 performers possible).

What would you do if your daughter ran away with the boyfriend from hell? Literally. If you are Demeter, the goddess of the harvest, you have the power to hold the whole earth hostage. One afternoon, Demeter's daughter Persephone is gathering flowers in a field with her mortal friends when she hears an otherworldly melody emanating from a cave. That evening, returning alone to seek the source of the music, she meets a mysterious young demigod who proves to be the nameless son of Hades, the lord of the dead. Drawn to his tales of a world of endless adventures, she follows him. Demeter comes in search of her and demands that she return home, now or never. But when Persephone refuses, Demeter likewise refuses to keep the seasons turning, threatening to destroy the mortal world with drought and famine...

The Unscary Ghost by Matt Buchanan

Comedy. 40-50 minutes. 3+ males, 5+ females, 8+ either (13-30+ performers possible).

Loosely based on Oscar Wilde's *The Canterville Ghost*. When the Otis family moves into the old Victorian home in Canterville, Ohio, they soon learn that the place is haunted. Only nobody in this jaded, modern family finds the ghost remotely frightening. The ghost, Simon Canter by name, is humiliated and frustrated by his attempts to live up to his assigned task of frightening people, while the family alternately taunts him and tries to exploit him, even trying to get a spot on the hit TV show, *America's Most Haunted*. Only the oldest daughter, Ginny, seems to care for or understand poor Simon. Can she help him find peace? A sometimes zany, sometimes touching show for the whole family.

The Wild and Wacky Rhyming Stories of Miss Henrietta Humpledowning by Tom Smith

Comedy. 35-45 minutes. 2-7 males, 2-11 females, 4+ either (8-22 performers possible).

Four strange, funny, and offbeat stories told in rhyming couplets. In *Dori Lee*, a girl's obsession with her looks goes too far. In *The Boy Who Grew a Tail*, a boy refuses to eat his vegetables—with dramatic results! In *The Bully, Earl Greene*, a girl wakes up in the body of the town bully, and in *The Giant Gnome*, young Zachary discovers you might not really want what you wish for. Reminiscent of the poetry of Shel Silverstein, and with a delightfully oddball bent!

Did you know that **www.youthplays.com** has dozens of monologues that are free for use in the classroom and for auditions? Go there today!

13534793R00033

Made in the USA
Charleston, SC
16 July 2012